Thematic Guide to Piano Literature

MARTHE MORHANGE-MOTCHANE

VOLUME IV
SCHUBERT / SCHUMANN

ED. 3291

G. Schirmer, Inc.
New York/London

VOLUME IV
SCHUBERT / SCHUMANN

This graded thematic guide of solo piano pieces is addressed to all lovers of music, and especially to piano teachers. The thematic presentation allows a rare and valuable overview of the work of the composer.

It is a selection of the basic piano literature: it does not encompass the complete works of all the composers included. But it does attempt to offer a wide variety of ways to arrange different programs for students of the same grade, taking into consideration their individual differences.

Proper grading is one of the most important elements of successful teaching and learning. The gradings proposed here always take into account the musical character of the piece as well as the technical problems involved.

The grading is aided by short comments which accompany the Mozart and Beethoven Sonatas, and the Chopin Preludes and Nocturnes. They point out, in each movement, the technical requirements, and the musical character determined by the piece. These brief indications imply an overall view of a piece; but because they cannot be precisely expressed in words they must rely also on images and impressions. These are, of course, subjective, and thus are always debatable.

Of course no gradings can be absolute; and the assignment of a grade does not mean that all pieces of the same grade are equally interchangeable. A choice must still be made according to the musical development, technical ability and maturity of the player.

In this guide nine grades are used. They correspond to the accepted divisions of difficulty:

Easy	Intermediate	Difficult	Advanced
I II	I II III	I II	I II

Compositions in Advanced II (for instance, the late Beethoven Sonatas), demand superior technique and great maturity. There is really no general way to decide when to confront them.

An overview of the music at each grade is given by the charts that precede the music.

I wish to thank Murray Present, professof ofmusic at Montclair State College, New Jersey, who shared his great knowledge of music in lucid and friendly discussions, for his constant encouragement. And Kathleen Giuffra Comini, piano teacher at the preparatory division of Montclair State College, who listened and questioned with great musical understanding, and my dear friend Anne Minor for unwavering confidence.

Marthe Morhange Motchane

Cette collection graduée de thèmes de la littérature du piano est dédiée à tous ceux qui aiment la musique et spécialement à ceux qui l'enseignent. La présentation thématique permet une vue d'ensemble rare et précieuse de l'oeuvre d'un compositeur.

C'est une sélection de base de la littérature pianistique qui, sans inclure l'oeuvre complète des compositeurs, propose un ensemble assez ample pour combiner un grand nombre de programmes variés et de differents degrés, ceci en tenant compte des différences individuelles des éxécutants ou élèves.

Bien graduer les oeuvres à choisir assure le succès de l'enseignement—et de tout apprentissage. La graduation adoptée traduit une recherche d'égalité entre les exigences du caractère musical de la pièce et de la technique pianistique.

L'appui de la graduation proposée est indiqué en de courts commentaires qui accompagnent les thèmes des Sonates de Beethoven et de Mozart, et des Preludes et Nocturnes de Chopin. Ces commentaires réunissent les exigences pianistiques les plus décisives et suggèrent le caractère musical qui doit diriger le travail technique. Ces indications sont nécessairement brèves et elles supposent toujours une certaine façon de comprendre la pièce: images et impressions sont inévitables et des avis différents toujours possibles.

En effet, aucune échelle de degré n'est absolue. Tel degré ne signifie pas non plus que toutes les pièces indiquées sont strictement interchangeables. Il reste encore des nuances et un choix peut encore s'imposer suivant le développement musical, les capacités de l'exécutant et sa maturité.

Las degrés s'échelonnent en partant des pièces dites les plus faciles de la littérature classique traditionnelle. Sont prévus neuf degrés:

Facile		Intermédiaire			Difficile		Avancé	
I	II	I	II	III	I	II	I	II

Les oeuvres marquées Avancé II exigent une grande maturité et compétence, par example, les dernières Sonates de Beethoven. On ne peut guère formuler de régles générales pour les aborder.

Des tableaux donnent un aperçu de tous les thèmes de chaque degré.

Ma reconnaissance va à Murray Present, professeur de musique au Monclair State College, New Jersey, qui m'a laissé partager sa grande connaissance de la musique dans des discussions lucides et amicales, pour son constant encouragement. A Kathleen Giuffra Comini, que enseigne à la Division Préparatoire au Montclair State College, qui a patiemment écouté, et soulevé des questions avec beaucoup de compréhension musicale, et mon amie chère,, Anne Minor, pour sa confiance qui n'a jamais fléchi.

Marthe Morhange Motchane

CONTENTS

Franz Schubert
(1797-1828)

Schubert wrote about four hundred ländlers, waltzes, minuettes and ecossaises. A selection of these was assembled for this volume.

The dances are very short. They are presented here in eight groups or chains. Each chain was assembled to suggest the unity of a composition. Modulation, contrasts and diversity of mood were among the main points in assembling the chains. Each chain may be performed as a miniature work of Schubert.

On connait de Schubert près de quartre cents Ländler, Valses, Menuets et Ecossaises. Ces danses sont des pièces très courtes.

Un choix est présenté ici en groupes ou chaines. Ce groupement suggère une certaine unité faite de rapports de modulations, de contrastes, accord ou diversité de caractères. Comme une oeuvre en miniature.

SCHUBERT

Le "Theme no." indique l'endroit de la pièce dans le texte.

Les nombres dans ce tableau indiquent les pièces ou mouvements de l'opus à gauche.

The "Theme Nos." show where the pieces are found in this book.

The numbers in the grading columns indicate the pieces/movements from the opus shown on the left.

Theme No.		Deutsch No.	Opus	Intermediate			Difficult	
				I	II	III	I	II
	Various Pieces							
1	Allegretto	915		Xc				
2	Andante	29			XC			
3–4	Two Scherzi	593			1B♭	2D♭		
5	Variations on a Waltz of Diabelli	718			XC			
6	March	606				XE		
7–12	6 Moments Musicaux	780	94	3f	1C 2A♭ 5f	4Ci	6A♭	
13–16	4 Impromptus	899	90			1C 3G♭	2E♭ 4A♭	
17–20	4 Impromptus	935	142			2A♭	1f 3B♭	4A♭
21–23	3 Piano Pieces	946				3C	1E♭ 2E♭	
26	13 Variations on Theme of Huttenbrenner	576					Xa	
25	10 Variations on an Original Theme	156						XF
24	Adagio and Rondo	545–6	145					XE
	Dances							
1–12	Chain 1, Twelve Ländlers	790	171			X		
13–26	Chain 2, Fourteen Waltzes	365	9			X		
27–38	Chain 3, Fifteen Waltzes and Ländlers	Various				X		
39–46	Chain 4, 8 Ecossaises, Ländlers, Waltzes	Various				X		
47–54	Chain 5, Eight Ländlers and Waltzes	Various				X		
55–61	Chain 6, Seven Minuets and Trios	Various				X		
62–65	Chain 7, Four Ländlers and Waltzes	Various			X			
66–75	Chain 8, Nineteen Waltzes and Ländlers	Various				X		

SCHUBERT SONATAS
(graded by movements)

Theme No.	Deutsch #	Op.	Key	Intermediate III	Difficult I	Difficult II	Advanced I
90	157		E	1, 2	3		
91	279		C	1, 2, 3			
78	557		A♭	1, 2, 3			
79	568	122	E♭	3	1, 2, 4		
82	664	120	A	2, 3	1		
92	566		e	1, 2	3		
84	845	48	a	1, 2	3	4	
76	459		E	3	1, 4	2, 5	
86	894	78	G	2, 3		4	1
81	625		f		1, 2, 3		
80	575	147	B		1, 2, 3	4	
89	960		B♭	3		1, 2, 4	
83	784	143	a		2		1, 3
77	537	164	a		2	1, 3	
87	958		c		2, 3	1	4
93	840		C			1, 2, 3, 4	
85	850	53	D			1, 3, 4	2
88	959		A			1, 2, 3, 4	
94	760	15	C			2	1, 3, 4

Sonata numbering in different editions

Deutsch #	157	279	459	537	557	566	568	575	625	664	760	784	840	845	850	894	958	959	960
Breitkopf	8	9	16	7	10	11	4	6		3	*	5	12	1	2		13	14	15
Universal			1	2			3	4	5	6	*	7	8	9	10	11	12	13	14
Schirmer			7				4	6		3	*	5		1	2		8	9	10
Peters			7				4	6		3	*	5		1	2	11	8	9	10

*Wanderer Fantasie, published separately

Various Pieces

1. Allegretto

D. 915 (1827)
C minor
Intermediate I

2. Andante

D. 29 (1812)
C
Intermediate II

3. Two Scherzi

D. 593 (1817)
No. 1
B♭
Intermediate II

4.

D. 593 (1817)
No. 2
D♭
Intermediate III

48413c

5.

Variation on a Waltz of Diabelli

D. 718 (1821)
C minor
Intermediate II

6.

March

Allegro con brio

D. 606 (1818)
E
Intermediate III

Trio

Trio in A♭

(p) legato sempre

stacc.

7.

Moments Musicaux, op. 94, D. 780

Moderato

op. 94, D. 780
No. 1
C
Intermediate II

8.

op. 94, D. 780
No. 2
A♭
Intermediate II

9.

op. 94, D. 780
No. 3
F minor
Intermediate I

10.

op. 94, D. 780
No. 4
C♯ minor
Intermediate III

11.

op. 94, D. 780
No. 5
F minor
Intermediate II

12.

op. 94, D. 780
No. 6
A♭
Difficult I

Four Impromptus, op. 90, D. 899

13.

op. 90, D. 899
No. 1
C minor
Intermediate III

14.

op. 90, D. 899
No. 2
E♭
Difficult I

15.

op. 90, D. 899
No. 3
G♭
Intermediate III

16.

op. 90, D. 899
No. 4
A♭
Difficult I

Four Impromptus, op. 142, D. 935

17.

op. 142, D. 935
No. 1
F minor
Difficult I

18.

op. 142, D. 935
No. 2
A♭
Intermediate III

19.

THEME
Andante

op. 142, D. 935
No. 3
B♭
Difficult I

20.

op. 142, D. 935
No. 4
A♭
Difficult II

Three Piano Pieces, D. 946 (1828)

21.

D. 946
No. 1
E♭ minor
Difficult I

22.

D. 946
No. 2
E♭
Difficult I

23. Allegro

D. 946
No. 3
C
Intermediate III

Adagio and Rondo

24. Adagio

op. 145, D. 545-6
E
Difficult II

10 Variations on an Original Theme

25. Andante

D. 156 (1815)
F
Intermediate (theme)
Difficult II (variations)

13 Variations on a Theme of Huttenbrenner

26. Andantino

D. 576 (1817)
A minor
Difficult I

Dances

(See note at beginning of section.)

Chain 1

Twelve Ländlers, op. 171, D. 790 (1823)

1.

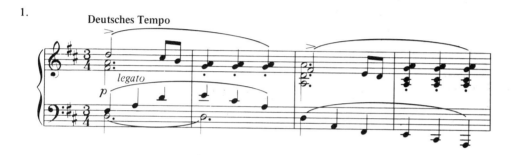

op. 171, D. 790
No. 1 in D
Intermediate III

2.

op. 171, D. 790
No. 2 in A
Intermediate III

3.

op. 171, D. 790
No. 3 in D
Intermediate III

4.

op. 171, D. 790
No. 4 in D
Intermediate III

48413

5.

op. 171, D. 790
No. 5 in B minor
Intermediate III

6.

op. 171, D. 790
No. 6 in G♯ minor
Intermediate III

7.

op. 171, D. 790
No. 7 in A♭
Intermediate III

8.

op. 171, D. 790
No. 8 in A♭ minor
Intermediate III

9.

op. 171, D. 790
No. 9 in B
Intermediate III

10.

op. 171, D. 790
No. 10 in B
Intermediate III

11.

op. 171, D. 790
No. 11 in A♭
Intermediate III

12.

op. 171, D. 790
No. 12 in E
Intermediate III

Chain 2

Fourteen Waltzes, op. 9, D. 365

13.

No. 1
op. 9/19, D. 365/19
G
Intermediate III

14.

No. 2
op. 9/20, D. 365/20
G
Intermediate III

15.

No. 3
op. 9/21, D. 365/21
G
Intermediate III

16.

No. 4
op. 9/22, D. 365/22
G♯ minor
Intermediate III

17.

No. 5
op. 9/23, D. 365/23
B
Intermediate III

18.

No. 6
op. 9/24, D. 365/24
B
Intermediate III

19.

No. 7
op. 9/25, D. 365/25
E
Intermediate III

20.

No. 8
op. 9/26, D. 365/26
E
Intermediate III

21.

No. 9
op. 9/27, D. 365/27
C♯ minor
Intermediate III

22.

No. 10
op. 9/28, D. 365/28
A
Intermediate III

18

23.

No. 11
op. 9/29, D. 365/29
D
Intermediate III

24.

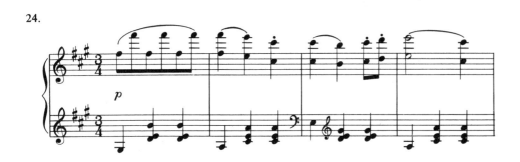

No. 12
op. 9/30, D. 365/30
A
Intermediate III

25.

No. 13
op. 9/31, D. 365/31
C
Intermediate III

26.

No. 14
op. 9/32, D. 365/32
F
Intermediate III

Chain 3

Twelve Waltzes and Ländlers

27.

No.1 Valses nobles
op. 77/11, D. 969/11
C
Intermediate III

28.

No.2 Waltz
op. 9/33, D. 365/33
F
Intermediate III

29.

**No.3
Valses sentimentales**
op. 50/19, D. 779/19
A♭
Intermediate III

30.

No.4 Waltz of Sadness
op. 9/2, D. 365/2
A♭
Intermediate III

31.

No.5 Waltz
op. 9/14, D. 365/14
D♭
Intermediate III

32.

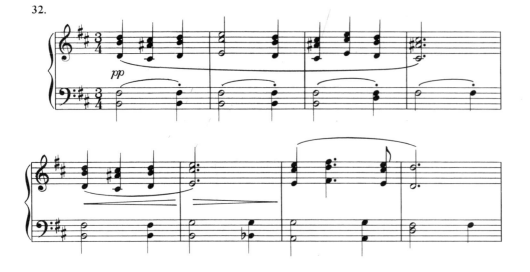

No. 6 Waltz
op. 18/10, D. 145/10
B minor
Intermediate III

Opus 171/1, D. 790/1, page **13**, and *Opus 171/2, D. 790/2*,
page **13** may be played here if desired.

33.

No. 7
Valses sentimentales
op. 50/3, D. 779/3
G
Intermediate III

34.

No. 8
Valses sentimentales
op. 50/1, D. 779/1
C
Intermediate III

35.

No. 9 Ländler
op. 171/3, D. 366/3
A minor
Intermediate III

36.

No. 10 Ländler
op. 171/4, D. 366/4
A minor
Intermediate III

37.

No. 11
Valses sentimentales
op. 50/13, D. 779/13
A
Intermediate III

38.

No. 12 Ländler
op. 67/8, D. 734/8
C
Intermediate III

48413

Chain 4

Eight Ecossaises, Ländlers and Waltzes

39.

No. 1 Ecossaise
op. 18/1, D. 145/1
A♭
Intermediate III

40.

No. 2 Ecossaise
op. 18/3, D. 145/3
D
Intermediate III

41.

No. 3 Ecossaise
op. 33/1, D. 783/1
B minor
Intermediate III

42.

No. 4 Last Waltzes
op. 127/1, D. 146/1
G
Intermediate III

43. **Trio**

No. 5 Last Waltzes
op. 127/5, D. 146/5
B♭
Intermediate III

44. **Trio**

No. 6 Last Waltzes
op. 127/9, D. 146/9
C
Intermediate III

45.

No. 7 Ländler
op. Posth., D. 366/15
D♭
Intermediate III

46.

No. 8 Ecossaise
Twelve Ecossaises, D. 299/5
D♭
Intermediate III

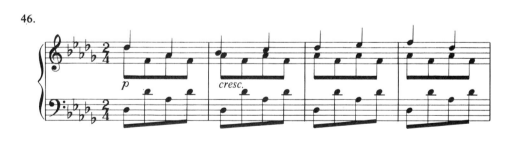

Chain 5

Eight Ländlers and Waltzes

47.

No. 1 German Dance
op. 33/2, D. 783/2
D
Intermediate III

48.

**No. 2
Valses sentimentales**
op. 50/12, D. 779/12
D
Intermediate III

49.

No. 3 Ländler
op. 67/5, D. 734/5
D
Intermediate III

50.

No. 4 Waltz
op. 18/6, D. 145/6
B minor
Intermediate III

51.

No. 5 Waltz
op. 18/8, D. 145/8
E♭ minor
Intermediate III

52.

No. 6 Waltz
op. 9/34, D. 365/34
F
Intermediate III

53.

No. 7 Waltz
op. 9/35, D. 365/35
F
Intermediate III

54.

No. 8 Waltz
op. 9/36, D. 365/36
F
Intermediate III

Opus Posth., *D. 366/15*, page **23**, and *12 Ecossaises, D. 299/5*,
page **23**, may be played here if desired.

Chain 6

Seven Minuets and Trios

55.

No. 1
D. 41/1
F
Intermediate III

56.

No. 2
D. 41/5
B♭
Intermediate III

57.

No. 3
D. 41/8
F
Intermediate III

Trio
D minor

58.

Minuet

No. 4
D. 41/10
B♭
Intermediate III

59.

Minuet

No. 5
D. 41/18
F
Intermediate III

60.

No. 6
D. 41/17
C
Intermediate III

61.

No. 7
D. 335/1&2
E
Intermediate III

Chain 7

Four Ländlers and Waltzes

62.

No. 1 Ländler
op. 18/3, D. 145/3
A♭
Intermediate II

63.

No. 2 Ländler
op. 67/3, D. 734/3
G
Intermediate II

64.

No. 3
Valses sentimentales
op. 50/18, D. 779/18
A♭
Intermediate II

65.

No. 4
Valses sentimentales
op. 50/27, D. 779/27
E♭
Intermediate II

48413

Chain 8

Ten Waltzes and Ländlers

66.

No. 1 Waltz
op. 18/5, D. 145/5
E minor
Intermediate III

67.

No. 2 Waltz
op. 18/9, D. 145/9
A
Intermediate III

68.

No. 3 German Dance
op. 33/5, D. 783/5
D
Intermediate III

69.

No. 4 German Dance
op. 33/11, D. 783/11
G
Intermediate III

70.

No. 5 Gräzer Waltz
op. 91/4, D. 924/4
A
Intermediate III

71.

No. 6 Waltz
D. 139
A
Intermediate III

72.

No. 7 Last Waltzes
op. 127/11, D. 146/11
B
Intermediate III

73.

No. 8 Ländler
D. 378/1
B
Intermediate III

74.

No. 9 Ländler
D. 378/5
B
Intermediate III

75.

No. 10 German Dance
D. 643
C minor
Intermediate III

Sonatas

Sonata in E, D. 459 (1816)

Published also as five "Klavierstücke"
The autograph with Sonate written on it was discovered later.
Publié aussi cinq "Klavierstücke"
L'autographe avec "Sonate" a été découvert plus tard.

76a.

Movement I
E
Difficult I

76b.

Movement II
E
Difficult II

76c.

Movement III
C
Intermediate III

76d.

Movement IV
A
Difficult I

76e.

Movement V
E
Difficult II (Advanced)

Sonata in A minor, op. 164, D. 537 (1817)

77a. Allegro ma non troppo

Movement I
A minor
Difficult II (Advanced)

77b. Allegretto quasi Andantino

Movement II
E
Difficult I

77c. Allegro vivace

Movement III
A minor
Difficult II

Sonata in A♭, D. 557 (1817)

78a.

Movement I
A♭
Intermediate III (Difficult I)

78b.

Movement II
E♭
Intermediate III (Difficult I)

78c.

Movement III
E♭
Intermediate III

Sonata in E♭, op. 122, D. 568 (1817)

79a.

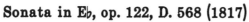

Movement I
E♭
Difficult I

79b. Andante molto

Movement II
G minor
Difficult I

79c. MENUETTO
Allegretto

Movement III
E♭
Intermediate III

79d. Allegro moderato

Movement IV
E♭
Difficult I

Sonata in B, op. 147, D. 575 (1817)

80a.   Allegro ma non troppo

Movement I
B
Difficult I

80b.   Andante

Movement II
E
Difficult I

Scherzo
Allegretto

80c.

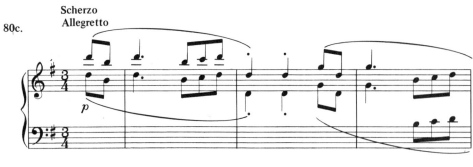

Movement III
G
Difficult I

80d.

Movement IV
B
Difficult II

Sonata in F minor, D. 625 (1818)

81a.

Movement I
F minor
Difficult I

81b¹.

Movement II
E
Difficult I

81b².

Trio
A

81c.

Movement III
F minor
Difficult I (II)

Sonata in A, op. 120, D. 664 (1825)

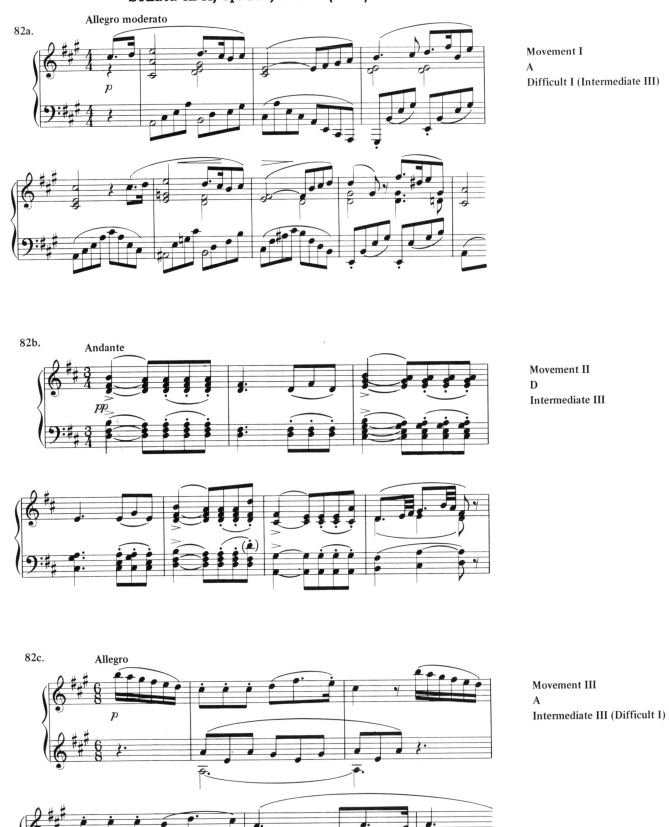

82a.

Allegro moderato

Movement I
A
Difficult I (Intermediate III)

82b.

Andante

Movement II
D
Intermediate III

82c.

Allegro

Movement III
A
Intermediate III (Difficult I)

Sonata in A minor, op. 143, D. 784 (1825)

83a. Allegro giusto

Movement I
A minor
Advanced

83b. Andante

Movement II
F
Difficult I

83c. Allegro vivace

Movement III
A minor
Advanced

Sonata in A minor, op. 42, D. 845 (1825)

84a. Moderato

Movement I
A minor
Intermediate III

84b. Andante poco moto

Movement II
C
Intermediate III

84c. SCHERZO
Allegro vivace

Movement III
A minor
Difficult I

84d. RONDO
Allegro vivace

Movement IV
A minor
Difficult II

48413

Sonata in D, op. 53, D. 850 (1825)

85a. **Allegro vivace**

Movement I
D
Difficult II

85b. **Con moto**

Movement II
A
Advanced

85c. **SCHERZO**
Allegro vivace

Movement III
D
Difficult II

85d. **RONDO**
Allegro moderato

Movement IV
D
Difficult II

48413

Sonata in G, op. 78, D. 894 (1825)

Also called Fantasia

86a. Molto moderato e cantabile

86b. Andante

MENUETTO
86c¹. Allegro moderato

86c². Trio

86d. Allegretto

Movement I
G
Advanced

Movement II
D
Intermediate III

Movement III
B minor
Intermediate III

Trio
B

Movement IV
G
Difficult II

48413

Sonata in C minor, Posth., D. 958 (1828)

87a.

Movement I
C minor
Difficult II (Advanced)

87b.

Movement II
Ab
Difficult I

MENUETTO

87c.

Movement III
C minor
Difficult I

87d.

Movement IV
C minor
Advanced

Sonata in A, Posth., D. 959 (1828)

88a.

Movement I
A
Difficult II (Advanced)

88b.

Movement II
F♯ minor
Difficult II (Advanced)

88c.

Movement III
A
Difficult II (Advanced)

88d.

RONDO
Allegretto

Movement IV
A
Difficult II (Advanced)

89a.

Sonata in B♭, Posth., D. 960 (1828)

Molto moderato

Movement I
B♭
Difficult II (Advanced)

89b.

Andante sostenuto

Movement II
C♯ minor
Difficult II (Advanced)

46

89c.

SCHERZO
Allegro vivace con delicatezza

Movement III
B♭
Intermediate III (Difficult I)

89d.

Allegro ma non troppo

Movement IV
B♭
Difficult II (Advanced)

Sonata in E, D. 157 (1815)
Incomplete Sonata but useful

90a.

Allegro ma non troppo

Movement I
E
Intermediate III

90b.

Movement II
E minor
Intermediate III

90c.

Movement III
B
Difficult I

91a.

Sonata in C, D. 279 (1815)

Unfinished

Movement I
C
Intermediate III

91b.

Movement II
F
Intermediate III

91c.

Movement III
A minor
Intermediate III

Sonata in E minor, D. 566 (1817)

92a.

Movement I
E minor
Intermediate III (Difficult I)

92b.

Movement II
E
Intermediate III (Difficult I)

92c.

Movement III
A♭
Difficult I

Sonata in C, D. 840 (1825)

93a.

Movement I
C
Difficult II

93b. Andante

Movement II
C minor
Difficult II

93c. MENUETTO
Allegretto

Movement III
A♭
Difficult II

93d. RONDO
Allegro

Movement IV
C
Difficult II

Wanderer Fantasia, op. 15, D. 760 (1822)

94a. Allegro con fuoco ma non troppo

Movement I
C
Advanced

94b. Adagio

Movement II
C♯ minor
Difficult II

94c. Presto

Movement III
A♭
Advanced

94d. Allegro

Movement IV
C
Advanced

Robert Schumann

(1810-1856)

SCHUMANN

Le "Theme no" indique l'endroit de la pièce dans le texte.
Les nombres dans ce tableau indiquent les pièces ou mouvements de l'opus à gauche.

The "Theme Nos." show where the pieces are found in the book.
The numbers in the grading columns indicate the pieces/movements from the opus shown on the left.

Theme No.		Op. No.	Easy		Intermediate			Difficult		Advanced	
			I	II	I	II	III	I	II	I	II
1–43	Album for the Young	68	1.2.3.4.5.	6.7.8.9.	10.12.14.16.19.	21.28.37.41.	13.15.17.22.25.	30.31.40. 42.			
				11.18.	20.23.24.		26.27.28.29.32.33.				
							34.35.36.38.39.43.				
44–55	Sonatas for the Young No. 1	118		Mov. 3	Mov. 1.2.4.						
	2					Mov. 1.3.4.	Mov. 2.				
	3					Mov. 1.2.3.4.	Mov. 1.				
56-69	Colored Leaves	99/I					1.	2.3.			
		II			1.3.5.	4.		2.			
		III					x.				
		IV				x.					
		V-VIII						x.			
70–82	Scenes from Childhood	15			1.	4.7.8.12.	2.5.6.9.10.13.	3.11.			
117–121	Morning Songs	133			1.	2.		3.4.5.			
103–111	Forest Scenes	82				1.3.5.6.	2.4.7.8.9.				
122–125	Night Pieces	23				4.		1.2	3.		
137	Variations on ABBEGG	1				2.	Theme	1.3.	4.5.		
112	Arabesque	18					x.				
114–116	Romances	28					1.2.	3.			
126–128	3 Fantasy Pieces	111					2.3.	1.			
129–136	Phantasie Pieces	12					1.3.	4.8.	2.5.6.	7.	
138–145	Novelettes	21					1.4.	5.6.	3.7.8.	2.	
146–157	Papillons	2					3,7.	1.	2.4.5.6.8.12.	9.10.11.	
83–102	Album Leaves	124			6.	4.5.7.11.13.	1.2.15.16.17.18.	3.8.9.10.12.1419.	20.		
158–162	Carnaval-Vienne	26					2.3.	1.4.	5.		
169–186	Davidsbündler	6					2.5.7.11.14.	18.	8.10.15.17.	1.3.4.9.	6.12.13.16
187–208	Carnaval	9					2.4.5.12.18.	3.11.13.16.19.	6.9.10.14.	1.7.8.15.	17.20.21.
210	Sonata	22					Mov. 2		Mov. 1.3	Mov. 4	
220	Phantasie	17					3.			1.	2.
234–238	Etudes Symphoniques	Posth.					4.	1.2.3.5.			
113	Blumenstück	19						x.			
163–168	Intermezzi	4						3.4.5.	6.	1.2.	
209	Sonata	11						Mov. 2.		Mov.3.	Mov. 1.4.
212–219	Kreisleriana	16						4.6.	2.5.7.8.	1.3.	
221–233	Symphonic Etudes	13						Theme 1.	2.	3.5.6.7.8.11.	4.9.10.12.
211	Sonata	14								Mov. 1.2.3.	Mov. 4.
239	Humoreske	20									x.
240	Toccata	7									x.

Album für die Jugend, op. 68
(Album for the Young)
(In order of difficulty)
(En ordre de difficulté)

A Little Piece
(Stückchen)

1.

op. 68, No. 5
C
Easy I

Melody
(Melodie)

2.

op. 68, No. 1
C
Easy I

Soldiers' March
(Soldatenmarsch)

3.

op. 68, No. 2
G
Easy I

Humming Song
(Trällerliedchen)

4.

op. 68, No. 3
C
Easy I

Chorale
(Ein Choral)

5.

op. 68, No. 4
G
Easy I

The Wild Rider
(Wilder Reiter)

6.

op. 68, No. 8
A minor
Easy II

48413c

Sicilienne
(Sizilianisch)

7.

Schalkhaft ♩. = 96
(Giocoso)

op. 68, No. 11
A minor
Easy II

The Poor Orphan
(Armes Waisenkind)

8.

Langsam ♪ = 108
(Lento)

op. 68, No. 6
A minor
Easy II

Hunting Song
(Jägerliedchen)

9.

Frisch und fröhlich ♩. = 116
(Lightly, with freshness)

op. 68, No. 7
F.
Easy II

A Little Folksong
(Volksliedchen)

10.

In Klagenden Ton ♩ = 92
(Doloroso)

op. 68, No. 9
D minor
Easy II

The Reapers' Song
(Schnitterliedchen)

11.

Nicht sehr schnell ♩. = 120
(Allegro ma non troppo)

op. 68, No. 18
C
Easy II

Little Study
(Kleine Studie)

12.

Leise und sehr egal zu spielen ♩. = 116
(lightly and always even)

op. 68, No. 14
G
Intermediate I

First Sorrow
(Erster Verlust)

13.

Nicht schnell ♩ = 96
(not fast)

op. 68, No. 16
E minor
Intermediate I

The Happy Farmer
(Fröhlicher Landmann)

14.

Frisch und munter ♩ = 116
(Animato e grazioso)

op. 68, No. 10
F
Intermediate I

Saint Nicolas
(Knecht Ruprecht)

15.

Allegro ♩ = 126

op. 68, No. 12
A minor
Intermediate I

48413

Rustic Song
(Ländliches Lied)

16.

Im mässigen Tempo ♩ = 104
(Moderato)

op. 68, No. 20
A
Intermediate I

Little Romance
(Kleine Romanze)

17.

Nicht schnell - not fast ♩ = 130
(not fast)

op. 68, No. 19
A minor
Intermediate I

Harvest Song
(Ernteliedchen)

18.

Mit fröhlichem Ausdruck ♩. = 80
(con gaia espressione)

op. 68, No. 24
A
Intermediate I

The Horseman
(Reiterstück)

19.

Kurz und bestimmt ♩. = 100
(Breve e deciso)

op. 68, No. 23
D minor
Intermediate I

Sailor's Song
(Matrosenlied)

20.

Nicht schnell ♩ = 136
(not fast)

op. 68, No. 37
G minor
Intermediate II

21.

(Untitled)

Langsam und mit Ausdruck zu spielen ♩ = 88
(Lento e con espressione)

op. 68, No. 21
C
Intermediate II

22.

Remembrance
(Erinnerung)

Nicht schnell und sehr gesangvoll zu spielen ♩ = 56
(Moderato e cantabile assai)

op. 68, No. 28
A
Intermediate II

23.

Norse Song
(Nordisches Lied)

Im Volkston ♩ = 92
(In modo popolare)

op. 68, No. 41
D minor
Intermediate II

24.

May, Sweet May
(Mai, lieber Mai)

Nicht schnell ♪ = 144
(not fast)

op. 68, No. 13
E
Intermediate III

48413

Roundelay
(Rundgesang)

25.

Massig. Sehr gebunden zu spielen ♩. = 72
(Moderato, legatissimo)

op. 68, No. 22
A
Intermediate III

Reminiscences of the Theatre
(Nachklänge aus dem Theater)

26.

Etwas agitiert ♩ = 100
(Un poco agitato)

op. 68, No. 25
A minor
Intermediate III

(Untitled)

27.

Nicht schnell, hübsch vorzutragen ♩ = 88
(Moderato, con grazia)

op. 68, No. 26
F
Intermediate III

The Little Morning Wanderer
(Kleiner Morgenwanderer)

28.

Frisch und kräftig ♪ = 126
(Animato ed energico)

op. 68, No. 17
A
Intermediate III

A Little Song in Canon-form
(Kanonisches Liedchen)

29.

Nicht schnell und mit innigem Ausdruck ♩ = 72
(Moderato e con intima espressione)

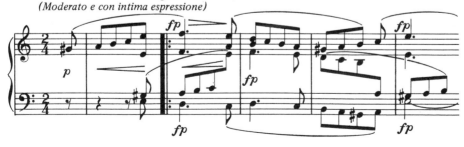

op. 68, No. 27
A minor
Intermediate III

The Stranger
(Fremder Mann)

30.

Stark und kräftig zu spielen ♩ = 144
(Forte ed energico)

op. 68, No. 29
D minor
Intermediate III

Sheherazade

31.

Ziemlich langsam, leise ♩ = 92
(somewhat slowly, and quietly)

op. 68, No. 32
A minor
Intermediate III

Spring Song
(Frühlingsgesang)

32.

Innig zu spielen ♩. = 56
(Con intimo sentimento)

op. 68, No. 15
E
Intermediate III

Harvest Time
(Weinlesezeit)

33.

Munter ♩ = 120
(Un poco animato)

op. 68, No. 33
E
Intermediate III

Theme

34.

Langsam. Mit inniger Empfindung ♪ = 84
(Lento con molto espressione)

op. 68, No. 34
C
Intermediate III

Mignon

35.

Langsam, zart ♩ = 104
(Lento e teneramente)

op. 68, No. 35
E♭
Intermediate III

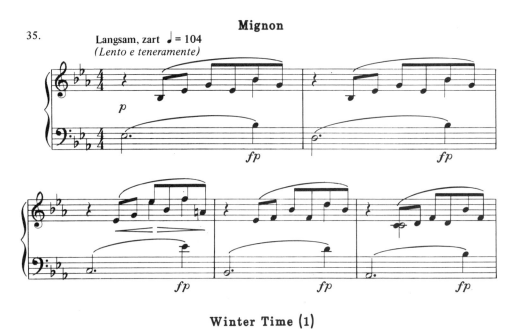

Winter Time (1)
(Winterzeit)

36.

Ziemlich langsam ♩ = 69
(Poco lento)

op. 68, No. 38
C minor
Intermediate III

Winter Time (2)
(Winterzeit)

New Year's Eve
(Sylvesterlied)

Italian Mariners' Song
(Lied italienischer Marinari)

War Song
(Kriegslied)

op. 68, No. 39
C minor
Intermediate III

op. 68, No. 43
A
Intermediate III

op. 68, No. 36
G minor
Intermediate III

op. 68, No. 31
D
Difficult I

(Untitled)

41.

Sehr langsam ♩ = 84
(Molto lento)

op. 68, No. 30
F
Difficult I

p Das zweite mal

Figured Chorale
(Figurierter Choral)

42.

Getragen ♩ = 92
(Sostenuto)

op. 68, No. 42
F
Difficult I

(p)

A Little Fugue
(Kleine Fuge)

43.

Vorspiel ♩ = 80
(Prelude)

op. 68, No. 40
A
Difficult I

p

FUGE

Lebhaft, doch nicht zu schnell ♩. = 88
(Vivace, ma non troppo)

p

p

p

50.

Langsam ♩ = 63
Lento

Movement III
(Evening Song)
(Abendlied)
G
Intermediate II

51.

Sehr lebhaft ♩ = 104
Assai vivace

Movement IV
(Children's Party)
(Kindergesellschaft)
D
Intermediate II

Sonata No. 3

(Dedicated to Mary)

52.

Allegro ♩ = 88
Tempo di marcia

Movement I
C
Intermediate II

53.

Ausdrucksvoll ♪ = 132
Espressivo

Movement II
(Andante)
F
Intermediate II

54.

Schnell ♩ = 80
Presto

Movement III
(Gypsy Dance)
(Zigeunertanz)
A minor
Intermediate II

55.

Sehr lebhaft ♩. = 126
Assai vivace

Movement IV
(A Child's Dream)
(Traum eines Kindes)
C
Intermediate II

Bunte Blätter, op. 99 (1839)
(Colored Leaves)
I. Drei Stücklein
(Three Small Pieces)

56.

Nicht schnell, mit Innigkeit
Non presto, con intimo sentimento

No. 1
A
Intermediate III

57.

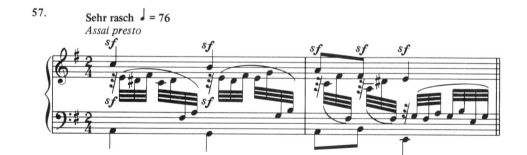

Sehr rasch ♩ = 76
Assai presto

No. 2
E minor
Difficult I

58.

Frisch ♩. = 116
Con freschezza

No. 3
E
Difficult I

II. Albumblätter
(Album Leaves)

59.

No. 1
F minor
Intermediate I

60.

No. 2
B minor
Difficult I

61.

No. 3
A♭
Intermediate I

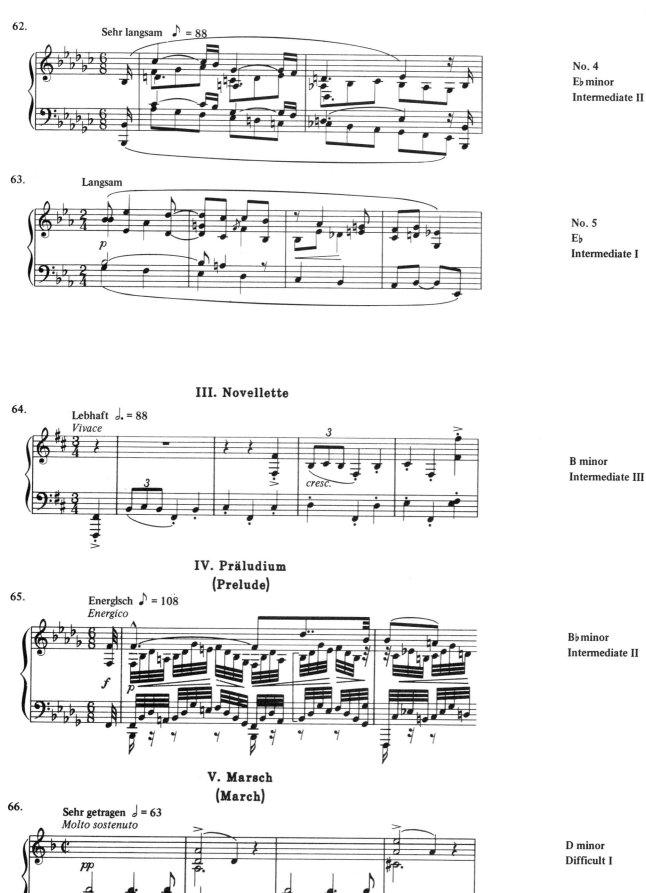

III. Novellette

IV. Präludium
(Prelude)

V. Marsch
(March)

48413

VI. Abendmusik
(Evening Music)

67.

Tempo di Minuetto ♩ = 120

B♭
Difficult I

VII. Scherzo

68.

Lebhaft ♩ = 160
Vivace

G minor
Difficult I

VIII. Geschwindmarsch
(Quick march)

69.

Sehr markiert ♩ = 108
Molto marcato

G minor
Difficult I

Scenes from Childhood, op. 15 (1838)
(Kinderszenen)

About Strange Lands and People
(Von fremden Ländern und Menschen)

70.

(Andantino) ♩ = 108

No. 1
G
Intermediate I

Curious Story
(Kuriose Geschichte)

71.

(Allegro Giocoso) ♩ = 112

No. 2
D
Intermediate III

72.

Blindman's Bluff
(Hasche-Mann)

(Allegro Scherzando) ♩ = 138

No. 3
B minor
Difficult I

73.

Pleading Child
(Bittendes Kind)

(Poco lento) ♪ = 138

No. 4
D
Intermediate II

74.

Perfectly Contented
(Glückes genug)

(Vivace Giocoso) ♪ = 132

No. 5
D
Intermediate III

75.

An Important Event
(Wichtige Begebenheit)

(Allegro Deciso) ♩ = 138

No. 6
A
Intermediate III

76.

Reverie
(Träumerei)

(Lento con espressivo) ♩ = 100

No. 7
F
Intermediate II

77.

At the Fireside
(Am Kamin)

(Allegretto) ♩ = 138

No. 8
F
Intermediate II

The Knight of the Rocking Horse
(Ritter vom Steckenpferd)

78.

(Allegro con brio) ♩. = 80

No. 9
C
Intermediate III

Almost too Serious
(Fast zu ernst)

79.

(Moderato, poco rubato) ♩ = 69

No. 10
G♯ minor
Intermediate III

Frightening
(Fürchtenmachen)

80.

(Poco Allegro) ♩ = 96

No. 11
G
Difficult I

Child Falling Asleep
(Kind im Einschlummern)

81.

(Lento non troppo) ♪ = 92

No. 12
E minor
Intermediate II

The Poet Speaks
(Der Dichter spricht)

82.

(Adagio espressivo) ♩ = 112

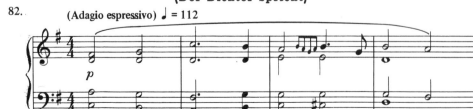

No. 13
G
Intermediate III

Albumblätter, op. 124
(Album Leaves)
20 Klavierstücke

Impromptu

83.

No. 1
F
Intermediate III

Presage of Sorrow
(Leides Ahnung)

84.

No. 2
A minor
Intermediate III

Scherzino

85.

No. 3
F
Difficult I

Waltz

86.

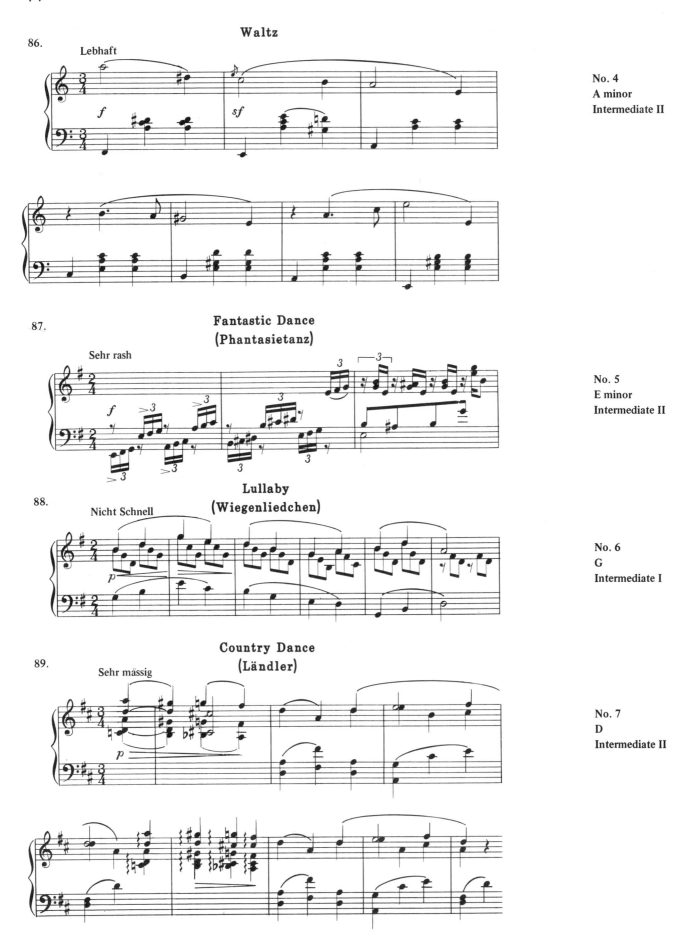

No. 4
A minor
Intermediate II

87. Fantastic Dance
(Phantasietanz)

No. 5
E minor
Intermediate II

88. Lullaby
(Wiegenliedchen)

No. 6
G
Intermediate I

89. Country Dance
(Ländler)

No. 7
D
Intermediate II

Larghetto

95.

No. 13
F minor
Intermediate II

Vision

96.

No. 14
F
Difficult I

Waltz

97.

No. 15
A♭
Intermediate III

Lullaby
(Schlummerlied)

98.

No. 16
E♭
Intermediate III

99.

The Elf
(Elfe)

So schnell als möglich

No. 17
A♭
Intermediate III

100.

A Message
(Botschaft)

Mit zartem Vortrag ♩ = 152

No. 18
E
Intermediate III

101.

Fantastic Piece
(Phantasiestück)

Leicht, etwas graziös ♩ = 76

No. 19
A
Difficult I

102.

Canon

Langsam ♩ = 84

No. 20
D
Difficult II

48413

Waldszenen, op. 82
(Forest Scenes)

Entrance
(Eintritt)

103.

No. 1
B♭
Intermediate II

Hunter in ambush
(Jäger auf der Lauer)

104.

No. 2
D minor
Intermediate III

Lonely Flowers
(Einsame Blumen)

105.

No. 3
B♭
Intermediate II

Haunted Spot
(Verrufene Stelle)

106.

No. 4
D minor
Intermediate III

Friendly Landscape
(Freundliche Landschaft)

107.

No. 5
B♭
Intermediate II

The Wayside Inn
(Herberge)

108.

No. 6
E♭
Intermediate II

48413

109.

The Prophetic Bird
(Vogel als Prophet)

Langsam, sehr zart
Lento

pp

No. 7
G minor
Intermediate III

110.

Hunting Song
(Jagdlied)

Rasch, kräftig ♩. = 120 (Animated with force)

No. 8
E♭
Intermediate III

111.

Departure
(Abschied)

Nicht schnell

p

mf

No. 9
B♭
Intermediate III

112.

Arabeske, op. 18

Leicht und zart ♩ = 108

p

p

C
Intermediate III

113.

Blumenstücke, op. 19
(Flower pieces)

♩ = 69

p

D♭.
Difficult I

Three Romances, op. 28 (1839)

114.

No. 1
Bb minor
Intermediate III

115.

No. 2
F#
Intermediate III

116.

No. 3
B
Difficult I

C# minor
Difficult I

Gesänge der Frühe, op. 133
(Morning Songs)

117.

No. 1
D
Intermediate I

118.

No. 2
D
Intermediate II

119.

No. 3
A
Difficult I

120.

No. 4
F♯ minor
Difficult I

121.

No. 5
D
Difficult I

Nachtstücke, op. 23 (1839)
(Night Pieces)

122. Mehr langsam, oft zurückhaltend ♩ = 100

No. 1
C
Difficult I

123. Markiert und lebhaft ♩ = 76

No. 2
F
Difficult I

124. Mit grosser Lebhaftigkeit ♩. = 72

No. 3
D♭
Difficult II

125. Ad libitum   Einfach ♩ = 96

No. 4
F
Intermediate II

Drei Phantasiestücke, op. 111 (1851)
(Three Fantasy Pieces)

126. Sehr rasch, mit leidenschaftlichem Vortrag ♩ = 84

No. 1
C minor
Difficult I

127. Ziemlich langsam ♩ = 72

No. 2
A♭
Intermediate III

128. Kräftig und sehr markiert ♩ = 96

No. 3
C minor
Intermediate III

Phantasiestücke, op. 12
(Fantasy Pieces)
In the Evening
(Des Abends)

No. 1
D♭
Intermediate III

Soaring
(Aufschwung)

No. 2
A♭
Difficult II

Why?
(Warum?)

No. 3
D♭
Intermediate III

Whims
(Grillen)

No. 4
D♭
Difficult I

In the Night (In der Nacht)

133.

Mit Leidenschaft ♩ = 126

No. 5
A♭
Difficult II

Fable (Fabel)

134.

Langsam ♩ = 48

No. 6
C
Difficult II

Schnell ♩ = 48

Dream Visions (Traumes Wirren)

135.

Auberst lebhaft ♩ = 160

No. 7
F
Advanced I

rit.

The End of the Song (Ende vom Lied)

136.

Mit guten Humor ♩ = 132

No. 8
F
Difficult I

Variations on the name "Abegg," op. 1 (1830)

Theme
F
Intermediate III

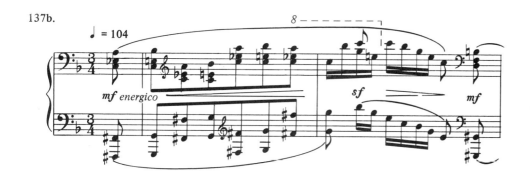

Variation I
F
Difficult I

Variation II
F
Intermediate II

48413

86

137d.

Variation III
F
Difficult I

137e.

Variation IV
(not numbered)
A♭
Difficult II

137f.

Finale
F
Difficult II

Noveletten, op. 21
(Novelettes)

138.
Markiert und kräftig

No. 1
F
Intermediate III

139.
Ausserst rasch mit Bravour (♩ = 92)

No. 2
D
Advanced I

140.
Leicht und mit Humor

No. 3
B minor
Difficult II

141.
Ballmäsig. Sehr munter

No. 4
D
Intermediate III

142.

Rauschend und festlich

No. 5
D
Difficult I

143.

Sehr lebhaft mit vielem Humor

No. 6
A
Difficult I

144.

Ausserst rasch

No. 7
E
Difficult II

145.

Sehr lebhaft

No. 8
F♯ minor
Difficult II

Papillons, op. 2 (1829–32)

146.

No. 1
D
Difficult I

147.

No. 2
E♭
Difficult II

148.

No. 3
F♯ minor
Intermediate III

149.

No. 4
A
Difficult II

No. 5
B♭
Difficult II

No. 6
D minor
Difficult II

152.

No. 7
F minor
Intermediate III

153.

No. 8
C♯ minor
Difficult II

154.

No. 9
B♭ minor
Advanced I

155.

No. 10
C
Advanced I

156.

No. 11
D
Advanced I

157.

No. 12
D
Difficult II

Faschingsschwank aus Wien, op. 26 (1839)
(Carnival in Vienna)

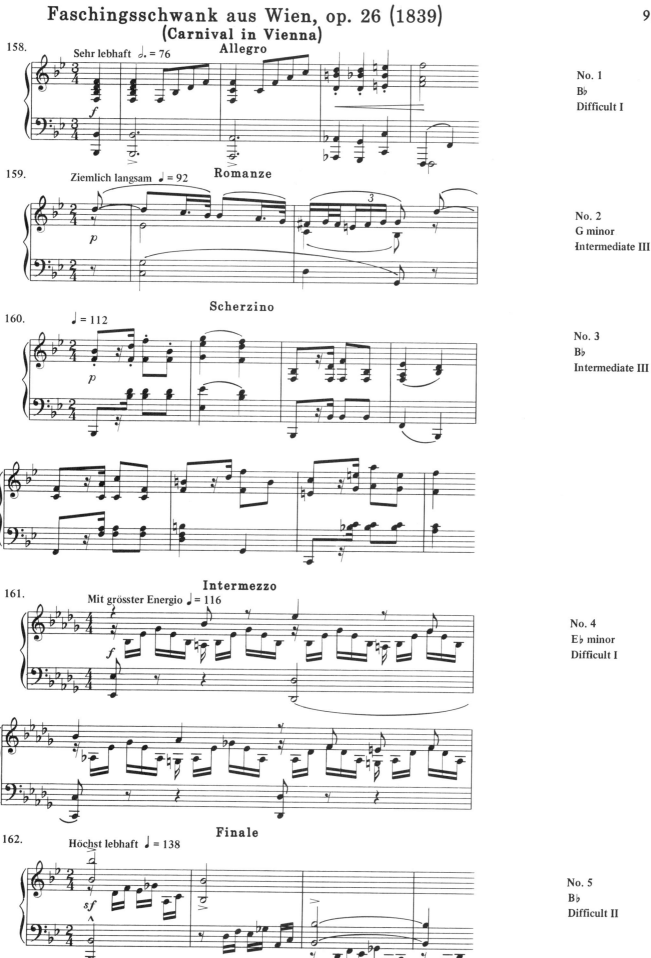

No. 1
Bb
Difficult I

No. 2
G minor
Intermediate III

No. 3
Bb
Intermediate III

No. 4
Eb minor
Difficult I

No. 5
Bb
Difficult II

48413

Intermezzi, op. 4 (1832)

163

No. 1
A
Advanced I

164.

No. 2
E minor
Advanced I

165.

No. 3
A minor
Difficult I

166.

No. 4
C
Difficult I

167.

No. 5
D minor
Difficult I

168.

No. 6
B minor
Difficult II

Davidsbündlertänze, op. 6 (1837)

18 character pieces dedicated to W. von Goethe.

169.

No. 1
G
Advanced I

170.

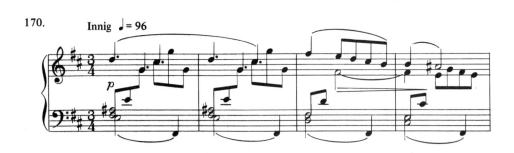

No. 2
B minor
Intermediate III

171.

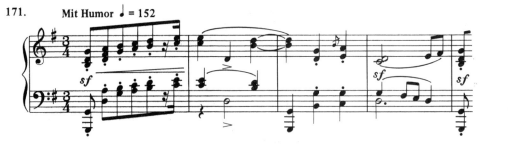

No. 3
G
Advanced I

172.

No. 4
B minor
Advanced I

181.

Wild und lustig ♩ = 152

No. 13
B minor
Advanced II

182.

Zart und singend ♩ = 100

No. 14
E♭
Intermediate III

183.

Frisch ♩. = 56

No. 15
B♭
Difficult II

Fine

100

184.

Mit gutem Humor ♩ = 132

p

f

No. 16
B minor
Advanced II

185.

Wie aus der Ferne ♩ = 100

p

No. 17
B
Difficult II

186.

Nicht schnell ♩ = 136

pp

No. 18
C
Difficult I

Carnaval, op. 9

Préambule

187.

No. 1
A♭
Advanced I

Pierrot

188.

No. 2
E♭
Intermediate III

Arlequin

189.

No. 3
B♭
Difficult I

Valse noble

190.

No. 4
Bb
Intermediate III

Eusebius

191.

No. 5
Eb
Intermediate III

Florestan

192.

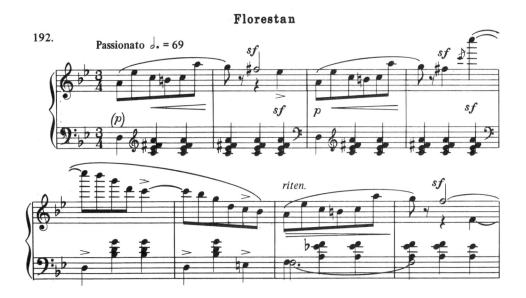

No. 6
Bb
Difficult II

193.

Coquette

Vivo ♩ = 176

pp

p

ff

p

No. 7
B♭
Advanced I

194.

Replique

L'istesso tempo

p

un poco con grazia

pp

(p)

riten.

No. 8
B♭
Advanced I

195.

Sphinxs

Sphinxs

196.

Papillons

Prestissimo ♩ = 152

sf

sf

No. 9
B♭
Difficult II

A.S.C.H. S.C.H.A.

197.

No. 10
(Lettres dansantes)
C minor
Difficult II

Chiarina

198.

No. 11
C minor
Difficult I

Chopin

199.

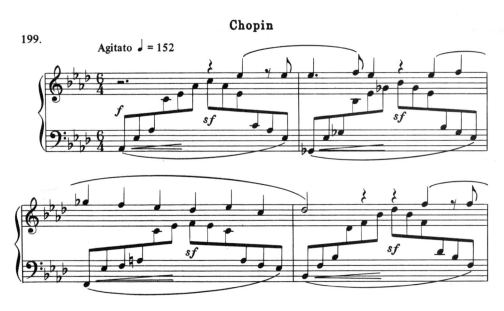

No. 12
A♭
Intermediate III

200.

Estrella

No. 13
F minor
Difficult I

201.

Reconnaissance

No. 14
A♭
Difficult II

202.

Pantalon et Colombine

No. 15
F minor
Advanced I

Valse Allemande

203.

No. 16
A
Difficult I

Paganini

204.

No. 17
Intermezzo:
Paganini
F minor
Advanced II

Aveu

205.

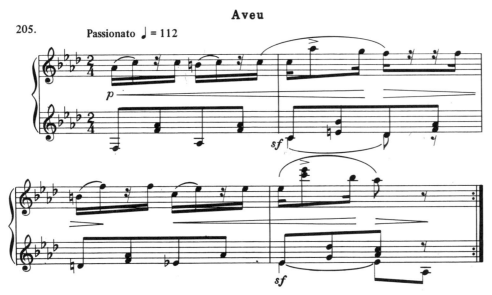

No. 18
F minor
Intermediate III

Promenade

206.

No. 19
Db
Difficult I

Pause

207.

No. 20
Ab
Advanced II

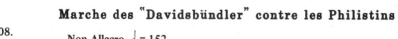

Marche des "Davidsbündler" contre les Philistins

208.

No. 21
Ab
Advanced II

Three Piano Sonatas
Grosse Sonate, op. 11
(Grand Sonata)

209a.

Movement I
F♯ minor
Advanced II

209b.

Movement II
A
Difficult I

209c.

Scherzo ed Intermezzo
Allegrissimo ♩ = 176

Movement III
F♯ minor
Advanced I

209d.

Finale
Allegro un poco maestoso ♩ = 116

Movement IV
F♯ minor
Advanced II

Zweite Sonate, op. 22 (1835-1838)

(Second Sonata)

210a.

So rasch wie möglich ♩ = 144

Movement I
G minor
Difficult II

110

210b.

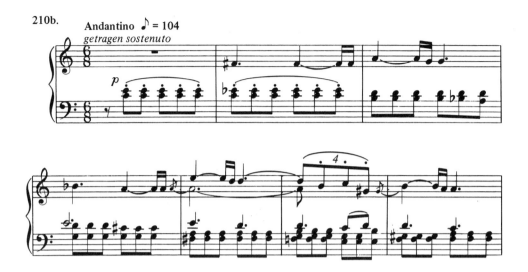

Movement II
C
Intermediate III

210c.

Movement III
G minor
Difficult II

Dritte Grosse Sonate, op. 14 (1835-53)

(Third Grand Sonata)

Kreisleriana, op. 16 (1838)

212.

No. 1
D minor
Advanced I

213.

No. 2
B♭
Difficult II

214.

No. 3
G minor
Advanced I

215. Sehr langsam ♪ = 66

No. 4
Bb
Difficult I

216. Sehr lebhaft ♩ = 160

No. 5
G minor
Difficult II

217. Sehr langsam ♪ = 108

No. 6
Bb
Difficult I

218.

Sehr rasch ♩ = 132
Molto presto

No. 7
C minor
Difficult II

219.

Schnell und spielend ♩. = 100

No. 8
G minor
Difficult II

Phantasie, op. 17 (1836)
(Fantasia)

220a.

Durchaus fantastisch und leidenschaftlich vorzutragen ♩ = 80

Movement I
C
Advanced I

220b.

Movement II
E♭
Advanced II

220c.

Movement III
C
Intermediate III

Symphonische Etuden, op. 13 (1834: rev. 1852)

Symphoniques Etudes en Forme de Variations
(Symphonic Etudes)

This work requires the most advanced technique and mature interpretation. Very difficult (constant light wrist action is required in Etudes III and IX).

Cette oeuvre demande une technique très avancée et une interprétation profonde et variée. Les études III et IX très difficiles exigent une action de poignet constante et lègér.

221.

Theme
C# minor
Difficult I

222.

Etude I
C# minor
Difficult I

223.

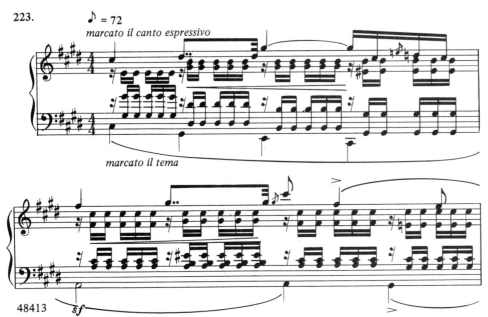

Etude II
C# minor
Difficult II

224.

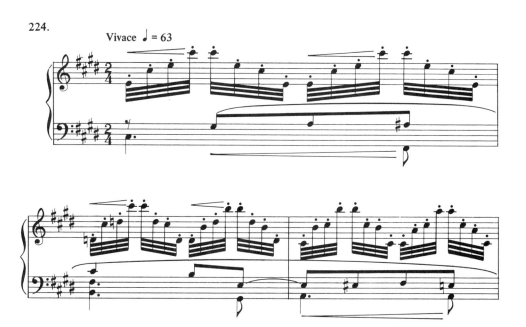

Vivace ♩ = 63

Etude III
C♯ minor
Advanced I

225.

♩ = 132

Etude IV
C♯ minor
Advanced II

226.

♩. = 108

Etude V
C♯ minor
Advanced I

227.

Etude VI
C♯ minor
Advanced I

228.

Etude VII
C♯ minor
Advanced I

229.

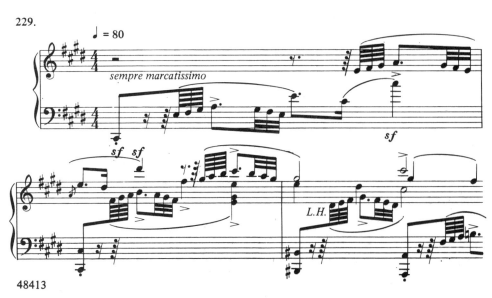

Etude VIII
C♯ minor
Advanced I

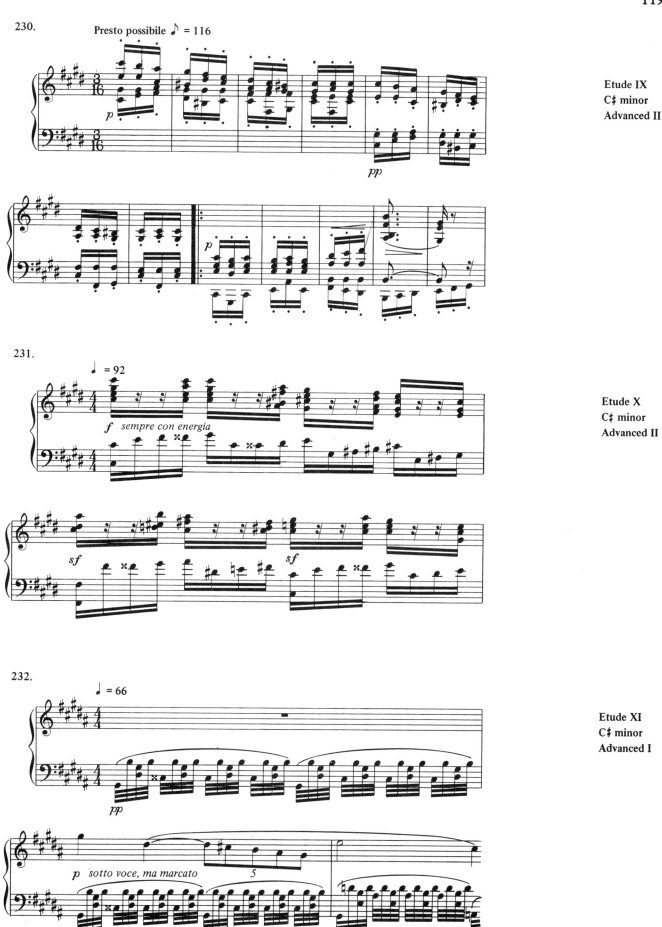

230.

Presto possibile ♪ = 116

Etude IX
C♯ minor
Advanced II

231.

♩ = 92

f sempre con energia

sf   sf

Etude X
C♯ minor
Advanced II

232.

♩ = 66

pp

p sotto voce, ma marcato   5

Etude XI
C♯ minor
Advanced I

Etudes Symphoniques Posthumes
(Variations posthumous)

These five etudes and the theme of Opus 13, make an attractive group. They are more difficult musically than technically.

Les cinq etudes et le thème de l'op. 13 font un bel ensemble plus difficile musicalement que techniquement.

Humoreske, op. 20 (1839)

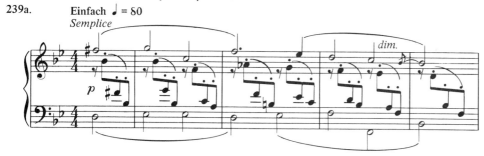

To be played without interruption. Very difficult musically and technically.

A jouer sans interruptions. Tres difficile musicalement et pianistiquement.

239a.

Einfach ♩ = 80
Semplice

(1)
B♭
Advanced II

239b.

Sehr zasch und leicht

(2)
B♭
Advanced II

239c.

Hastig ♩ = 126
Affrettato

Inner Stimme (Voce intimo)

(3)
G minor
Advanced II

239d. **Einfach und zart** ♩ = 100
Semplice, teneramente

(4)
G minor
Advanced II

239e. **Innig** ♩ = 116
Con intima expressione

(5)
B♭
Advanced II

239f. **Sehr lebhaft** ♩ = 76
Assai vivace

(6)
G minor
Advanced II

239g.

(7)
In conclusion
(Zum Beschluss)
G minor
Advanced II

Toccata, op. 7 (1833)

240.

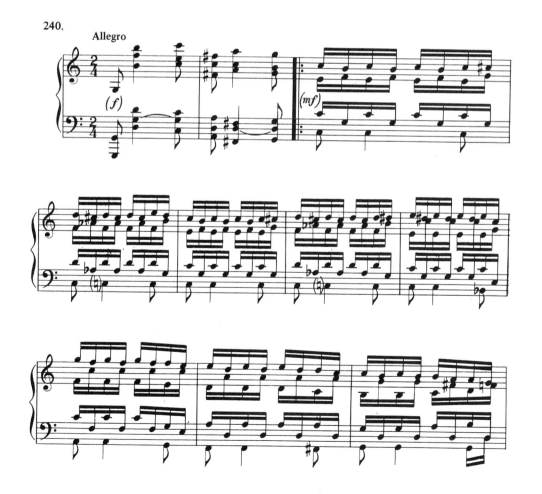

C
Advanced II

Thematic Index

SCHUBERT: VARIOUS PIECES

Theme No.	Title	Deutsch No.	Opus No.	Key	Intermediate I	II	III	Difficult I	II
1	Allegretto	915		c	x				
2	Andante	29		C		x			
3	Two Scherzi—No. 1	593		Bb		x			
4	2	593		Db			x		
5	Variations on a Waltz of Diabelli	718		c		x			
6	March	606		E			x		
	Moments Musicaux	780	94						
7	No. 1			C		x			
8	2			Ab		x			
9	3			f	x				
10	4			c#			x		
11	5			f		x			
12	6			Ab				x	
	Four Impromptus	899	90						
13	No. 1			c			x		
14	2			Eb				x	
15	3			Gb			x		
16	4			Ab				x	
	Four Impromptus	935	142						
17	No. 1			f				x	
18	2			Ab			x		
19	3			Bb				x	
20	4			Ab					x
	Three Piano Pieces	946							
21	No. 1			Eb				x	
22	2			Eb				x	
23	3			C			x		
24	Adagio and Rondo	545-6	145	E					x
25	10 Variations on an Original Theme	156		F					x
26	13 Variations on a Theme of Huttenbrenner	576		a				x	

SCHUBERT DANCES

Theme No.	Title	Henle Deutsch No.	Opus No.	Key	Intermediate II	III
	CHAIN 1: Twelve Ländlers	790/	171/			
1	No. 1	1	1	D		x
2	2	2	2	A		x
3	3	3	3	D		x
4	4	4	4	D		x
5	5	5	5	b		x
6	6	6	6	g♯		x
7	7	7	7	A♭		x
8	8	8	8	A♭		x
9	9	9	9	B		x
10	10	10	10	B		x
11	11	11	11	A♭		x
12	12	12	12	E		x
	CHAIN 2: Fourteen Waltzes	365/	9/			
13	1	19	19	G		x
14	2	20	20	G		x
15	3	21	21	G		x
16	4	22	22	g♯		x
17	5	23	23	B		x
18	6	24	24	B		x
19	7	25	25	E		x
20	8	26	26	E		x
21	9	27	27	c♯		x
22	10	28	28	A		x
23	11	29	29	D		x
24	12	30	30	A		x
25	13	31	31	C		x
26	14	32	32	F		x
	CHAIN 3: Twelve Waltzes and Ländlers					
27	No. 1. Valse nobles	969/11	77/11	C		x
28	2. Waltz	365/33	9/33	F		x
29	3. Valses sentimentales	779/19	50/19	A♭		x
30	4. Waltz of sadness	365/2	9/2	A♭		x
31	5. Waltz	365/14	9/14	D♭		x
32	6. Waltz	145/10	18/10	b		x
33	7. Valses sentimentales	779/3	50/3	G		x
34	8. Valses sentimentales	779/1	50/1	C		x
35	9. Ländler	366/3	171/3	a		x
36	10. Ländler	366/4	171/4	a		x
37	11. Valses sentimentales	779/13	50/13	A		x
38	12. Ländler	734/8	67/8	C		x

Theme No.	Title	Henle Deutsch No.	Opus No.	Key	Intermediate II	III
	CHAIN 4: Eight Ecossaises, Ländlers, Waltzes					
39	No. 1. Ecossaise	145/1	18/1	A♭		x
40	2. Ecossaise	145/3	18/3	D		x
41	3. Ecossaise	783/1	33/1	b		x
42	4. Last Waltzes	146/1	127/1	G		x
43	5. Last Waltzes	146/5	127/5	B♭		x
44	6. Last Waltzes	146/9	127/9	C		x
45	7. Ländler	366/15		D♭		x
46	8. Ecossaise (Twelve Ecossaises)	299/5		D♭		x
	CHAIN 5: Eight Ländlers and Waltzes					
47	No. 1. German Dance	783/2	33/2	D		x
48	2. Valses sentimentales	779/12	50/12	D		x
49	3. Ländler	734/5	67/5	D		x
50	4. Waltz	145/6	18/6	b		x
51	5. Waltz	145/8	18/8	e♭		x
52	6. Waltz	365/34	9/34	F		x
53	7. Waltz	365/35	9/35	F		x
54	8. Waltz	365/36	9/36	F		x
	CHAIN 6: Seven Minuets and Trios					
55	No. 1. Minuet and Trio	41/1		F		x
56	2. Minuet and Trio	41/5		B♭		x
57	3. Minuet	41/9		F		x
	Trio	41/9		d		x
58	4. Minuet and Trio	41/10		B♭		x
59	5. Minuet and Trio	41/18		F	x	
60	6. Minuet and Trio	41/17		C		x
61	7. Minuet and Trio	335/1&2		E		x
	CHAIN 7: Four Ländlers and Waltzes					
62	No. 1. Ländler	145/3	18/3	A♭	x	
63	2. Ländler	734/3	67/3	G	x	
64	3. Valses sentimentales	779/18	50/18	A♭	x	
65	4. Valses sentimentales	779/27	50/27	E♭	x	
	CHAIN 8: Ten Waltzes and Ländlers					
66	No. 1. Waltz	145/5	18/5	e		x
67	2. Waltz	145/9	18/9	A		x
68	3. German Dance	783/5	33/5	D		x
69	4. German Dance	783/11	33/11	G		x
70	5. Gräzer Waltz	924/4	91/4	A		x
71	6. Waltz	139		A		x
72	7. Last Waltzes	146/11	127/11	B♭		x
73	8. Ländler	378/1		B♭		x
74	9. Ländler	378/5		B♭		x
75	10. German Dance	643		c♯		x

Note: Most of the above pieces can be found in Schirmer Library No. 1537

SCHUBERT: PIANO SONATAS
(Sonatas Are Graded by Movements)

	Sonata Deutsch #	Opus #	Key	Breitkopf	Universal	Schirmer	Peters	Intermediate III	Difficult I	Difficult II	Advanced I
76	459	—	E	16	1	—	—	3	1,4	2,5	(5)
77	537	164	a	7	2	7	7		2	1,3	(1)
78	557	—	A♭	10	—	—	—	1,2,3	(1,2)		
79	568	122	E♭	4	3	4	4	3	1,2,4		
80	575	147	B	6	4	6	6		1,2,3	4	
81	625	—	f	—	5	—	—		1,2,3	(3)	
82	664	120	A	3	6	3	3	(1),2,3	1,(3)		
83	784	143	a	5	7	5	5		2		1,3
84	845	42	a	1	9	1	1	1,2	3	4	
85	850	53	D	2	10	2	2			1,3,4	2
86	894	78	G	—	11	—	11	2,3		4	1
87	958	Posth.	c	13	12	8	8		2,3	1	(1),4
88	959	Posth.	A	14	13	9	9			1,2,3,4	(1,2,3,4)
89	960	Posth.	B♭	15	14	10	10	3		1,2,4	(1,2,4)
90	157	—	E	8	—	—	—	1,2	3		
91	279	—	C	9	—	—	—	1,2,3			
92	566	—	e	11	—	—	—	1,2	(1,2),3		
93	840	—	C	12	8	—	—			1,2,3,4	
94	Wanderer Fantasia										
	760	15	C	—	—	—	—			2	1,3,4

SCHUMANN

Theme No.	Title	Key	Easy I	Easy II	Intermediate I	Intermediate II	Intermediate III	Difficult I	Difficult II	Advanced I	Advanced II
	Album for the Young, op. 68										
1	No. 5,* A Little Piece	C	x								
2	No. 1, Melody	C	x								
3	No. 2, Soldiers' March	G	x								
4	No. 3, Humming Song	C	x								
5	No. 4, Chorale	G	x								
6	No. 8, The Wild Rider	a		x							
7	No. 11, Sicilienne	a		x							
8	No. 6, The Poor Orphan	a		x							
9	No. 7, Hunting Song	F		x							
10	No. 9, A Little Folksong	d		x							
11	No. 18, The Reapers' Song	C		x							
12	No. 14, Little Study	G			x						
13	No. 16, First Sorrow	e			x						
14	No. 10, The Happy Farmer	F			x						
15	No. 12, Knecht Ruprecht	a			x						
16	No. 20, Rustic Song	A			x						
17	No. 19, Little Romance	a			x						
18	No. 24, Harvest Song	A			x						
19	No. 23, The Horseman	d			x						
20	No. 37, Sailor's Song	g				x					
21	No. 21, Untitled	C				x					
22	No. 28, Remembrance	A				x					
23	No. 41, Norse Song	d				x					
24	No. 13, May, Sweet May	E					x				
25	No. 22, Roundelay	A					x				
26	No. 25, Reminiscences of the Theatre	a					x				
27	No. 26, Untitled	F					x				
28	No. 17, The Little Morning Wanderer	A					x				
29	No. 27, A Little Song in Canon-form	a					x				
30	No. 29, The Stranger	d					x				
31	No. 32, Sheherazade	a					x				
32	No. 15, Spring Song	E					x				
33	No. 33, Harvest-Time	E					x				
34	No. 34, Theme	C					x				
35	No. 35, Mignon	E♭					x				
36	No. 38, Winter Time (1)	c					x				
37	No. 39, Winter Time (2)	c					x				
38	No. 43, New Year's Eve	A					x				
39	No. 36, Italian Mariners' Song	g					x				

*Schumann's numbering of the pieces

SCHUMANN

Theme No.	Title	Key	Easy I	Easy II	Intermediate I	Intermediate II	Intermediate III	Difficult I	Difficult II	Advanced I	Advanced II
40	No. 31, War Song	D						x			
41	No. 30, Untitled	F						x			
42	No. 42, Figured Chorale	F						x			
43	No. 40, A Little Fugue	A						x			
	Three Sonatas for the Young, Op. 118										
	Sonata No. 1—										
44	M. I	G			x						
45	II (Theme and Variations)	e			x						
46	III (Doll's Lullaby)	c		x							
47	IV (Rondoletto)	G			x						
	Sonata No. 2—										
48	M. I	D				x					
49	II (Canon)	b					x				
50	III (Evening Song)	G				x					
51	IV (Children's Party)	D				x					
	Sonata No. 3—										
52	M. I	C				x	(x)				
53	II (Andante)	F				x					
54	III (Gypsy Dance)	a				x					
55	IV (A Child's Dream)	C				x					
	Bunte Blätter, Op. 99 (Colored Leaves)										
56	I. Three Small Pieces—No. 1	A					x				
57	2	e						x			
58	3	E						x			
59	II. Album Leaves—No. 1	f			x						
60	2	b						x			
61	3	A♭			x						
62	4	e♭				x					
63	5	E♭			x						
64	III. Novellette	b					x				
65	IV. Prelude	b♭				x					
66	V. March	d						x			
67	VI. Evening Music	B♭						x			
68	VII. Scherzo	g						x			
69	VIII. Quick March	g						x			
	Kinderszenen, Op. 15 (Scenes from Childhood)										
70	No. 1, About Strange Lands and People	G			x						
71	No. 2, Curious Story	D					x				
72	No. 3, Blindman's Bluff	b						x			
73	No. 4, Pleading Child	D				x					

Theme No.	Title	Key	Easy I	Easy II	Intermediate I	Intermediate II	Intermediate III	Difficult I	Difficult II	Advanced I	Advanced II
74	No. 5, Perfectly Contented	D					x				
75	No. 6, An Important Event	A					x				
76	No. 7, Reverie	F				x					
77	No. 8, At the Fireside	F				x					
78	No. 9, The Knight of the Rocking Horse	C					x				
79	No. 10, Almost too Serious	g♯					x				
80	No. 11, Frightening	G						x			
81	No. 12, Child Falling Asleep	e				x					
82	No. 13, The Poet Speaks	G					x				
	Albumblätter, Op. 124 (Album Leaves)										
83	No. 1, Impromptu	F					x				
84	No. 2, Presage of Sorrow	a					x				
85	No. 3, Scherzino	F						x			
86	No. 4, Waltz	a				x					
87	No. 5, Fantastic Dance	e				x					
88	No. 6, Lullaby	G			x						
89	No. 7, Country Dance	D				x					
90	No. 8, Song Without End	F						x			
91	No. 9, Impromptu	B♭						x			
92	No. 10, Waltz	E♭						x			
93	No. 11, Romance	B♭				x					
94	No. 12, Burlesque	A♭						x			
95	No. 13, Larghetto	f				x					
96	No. 14, Vision	F						x			
97	No. 15, Waltz	A♭					x				
98	No. 16, Lullaby	E♭					x				
99	No. 17, The Elf	A♭					x				
100	No. 18, A Message	E					x				
101	No. 19, Fantastic Piece	A						x			
102	No. 20, Canon	D							x		
	Waldszenen, Op. 82 (Forest Scenes)										
103	No. 1, Entrance	B♭				x					
104	No. 2, Hunter in Ambush	d					x				
105	No. 3, Lonely Flowers	B♭				x					
106	No. 4, Haunted Spot	d					x				
107	No. 5, Friendly Landscape	B♭				x					
108	No. 6, The Wayside Inn	E♭				x					
109	No. 7, The Prophetic Bird	g					x				
110	No. 8, Hunting Song	E♭					x				
111	No. 9, Departure	B♭					x				
112	Arabeske Op. 18	C					x				
113	Blumenstücke, Op. 19	D♭						x			

Theme No.	Title	Key	Easy I	Easy II	Intermediate I	Intermediate II	Intermediate III	Difficult I	Difficult II	Advanced I	Advanced II
	Three Romances, Op. 28										
114	No. 1	b♭					x				
115	2	F♯					x				
116	3	B/c♯						x			
	Morning Songs, Op. 133										
117	No. 1	D		x							
118	2	D			x						
119	3	A						x			
120	4	f♯						x			
121	5	D						x			
	Nachtstücke, Op. 23										
122	No. 1	C						x			
123	2	F						x			
124	3	D♭							x		
125	4	F			x						
	Drei Phantasiestücke, Op. 111										
126	No. 1	c						x			
127	2	A♭					x				
128	3	c					x				
	Phantasiestücke, Op. 12										
129	No. 1, Evening	D♭					x				
130	No. 2, Soaring	A♭							x		
131	No. 3, Why?	D♭					x				
132	No. 4, Whims	D♭						x			
133	No. 5, In the Night	A♭							x		
134	No. 6, Fable	C							x		
135	No. 7, Dream Visions	F								x	
136	No. 8, End of the Song	F						x			
	Variations on the name "Abegg", Op. 1										
137a	Theme	F					x				
b	Var. I	F						x			
c	Var. II	F			x						
d	Var. III	F						x			
e	Var. IV	A♭							x		
f	Finale	F							x		
	Noveletten, Op. 21										
138	No. 1	F					x				
139	2	D								x	
140	3	b							x		
141	4	D					x				
142	5	D						x			
143	6	A						x			

Theme No.	Title	Key	Easy I	Easy II	Intermediate I	Intermediate II	Intermediate III	Difficult I	Difficult II	Advanced I	Advanced II
144	7	E							x		
145	8	f♯							x		
	Papillons, Op. 2										
146	No. 1	D						x			
147	2	E♭							x		
148	3	f♯				x					
149	4	A							x		
150	5	B♭							x		
151	6	d							x		
152	7	f				x					
153	8	c♯							x		
154	9	b♭								x	
155	10	C								x	
156	11	D								x	
157	12	D						x			
	Carnival in Vienna, Op. 26										
158	No. 1, Allegro	B♭						x			
159	No. 2, Romance	g				x					
160	No. 3, Scherzino	B♭				x					
161	No. 4, Intermezzo	e♭						x			
162	No. 5, Finale	B♭							x		
	Intermezzi, Op. 4										
163	No. 1	A								x	
164	2	e								x	
165	3	a						x			
166	4	C						x			
167	5	d						x			
168	6	b							x		
	Davidsbündlertänze, Op. 6										
169	No. 1	G								x	
170	2	b				x					
171	3	G								x	
172	4	b								x	
173	5	D				x					
174	6	d									x
175	7	g				x					
176	8	c							x		
177	9	C								x	
178	10	d						x			
179	11	b				x					
180	12	e									x
181	13	b									x
182	14	E♭					x				

Theme No.	Title	Key	Easy I	Easy II	Intermediate I	Intermediate II	Intermediate III	Difficult I	Difficult II	Advanced I	Advanced II
183	15	B♭							x		
184	16	b									x
185	17	B						x			
186	18	C					x				
	Carnaval, Op. 9										
187	No. 1, Préamble	A♭								x	
188	No. 2, Pierrot	E♭				x					
189	No. 3, Arlequin	B♭					x				
190	No. 4, Valse noble	B♭				x					
191	No. 5, Eusebius	E♭				x					
192	No. 6, Florestan	B♭							x		
193	No. 7, Coquette	B♭								x	
194	No. 8, Replique	B♭								x	
195	Sphinxs										
196	No. 9, Papillons	B♭							x		
197	No. 10, A.S.C.H. S.C.H.A.	c							x		
198	No. 11, Chiarina	c						x			
199	No. 12, Chopin	A♭				x					
200	No. 13, Estrella	f						x			
201	No. 14, Reconnaissance	A♭							x		
202	No. 15, Pantalon et Colombine	f								x	
203	No. 16, Valse Allemande	A♭						x			
204	No. 17, Intermezzo: Paganini	f									x
205	No. 18, Aveu	f				x					
206	No. 19, Promenade	D♭						x			
207	No. 20, Pause	A♭									x
208	No. 21, Marche des "Davidsbündler" contre les Philistines	A♭									x
	Three Piano Sonatas										
	Grosse Sonate, Op. 11										
209a	M. I	f♯									x
b	M. II	A						x			
c	M. III	f♯								x	
d	M. IV	f♯									x
	Zweite Sonate, Op. 22										
210a	M. I	g							x		
b	M. II	C				x					
c	M. III	g							x		
d	M. IV	B♭								x	
	Dritte Grosse Sonate, Op. 14										
211a	M. I	f								x	
b	M. II	D								x	
c	M. III	f								x	
d	M. IV	f									x

Theme No.	Title	Key	Easy		Intermediate			Difficult		Advanced	
			I	II	I	II	III	I	II	I	II
	Kreisleriana, Op. 10										
212	No. 1	d								x	
213	2	B♭							x		
214	3	g								x	
215	4	B♭						x			
216	5	g							x		
217	6	B♭						x			
218	7	c							x		
219	8	g							x		
	Phantasie, Op. 17										
220a	M. I	C								x	
b	M. II	E♭									x
c	M. III	C					x				
	Symphonic Etudes, Op. 13 (in variation form)										
221	Theme	c♯						x			
222	Etude I	c♯						x			
223	II	c♯							x		
224	III	c♯								x	
225	IV	c♯									x
226	V	c♯								x	
227	VI	c♯								x	
228	VII	c♯								x	
229	VIII	c♯								x	
230	IX	c♯									x
231	X	c♯									x
232	XI	c♯								x	
233	XII (Finale)	c♯									x
	Etudes Symphoniques Posthumous										
234	Etude I	c♯						x			
235	II	c♯						x			
236	III	c♯						x			
237	IV	c♯					x				
238	V	D♭						x			
	Humoreske, Op. 20										
239a	(1)	B♭									x
b	(2)	B♭									x
c	(3)	g									x
d	(4)	g									x
e	(5)	B♭									x
f	(6)	g									x
g	(7)	g									x
240	Toccata, Op. 7	C									x

Easy Intermediate Difficult Advanced